Student of Life

– Begin

Student of Life

Have you found what you're looking for?

– Begin

TONY J BOSNJAK

BALBOA.
PRESS

A DIVISION OF HAY HOUSE

Balboa Press books may be ordered through booksellers or by contacting:

Balboa Press
A Division of Hay House
1663 Liberty Drive
Bloomington, IN 47403
www.balboapress.com
1 (877) 407-4847

Because of the dynamic nature of the Internet, any web addresses or links contained in this book may have changed since publication and may no longer be valid. The views expressed in this work are solely those of the author and do not necessarily reflect the views of the publisher, and the publisher hereby disclaims any responsibility for them.

The author of this book does not dispense medical advice or prescribe the use of any technique as a form of treatment for physical, emotional, or medical problems without the advice of a physician, either directly or indirectly. The intent of the author is only to offer information of a general nature to help you in your quest for emotional and spiritual well-being. In the event you use any of the information in this book for yourself, which is your constitutional right, the author and the publisher assume no responsibility for your actions.

Any people depicted in stock imagery provided by Thinkstock are models, and such images are being used for illustrative purposes only.
Certain stock imagery © Thinkstock.

Printed in the United States of America.

ISBN: 978-1-4525-6107-3 (sc)
ISBN: 978-1-4525-6108-0 (e)

Library of Congress Control Number: 2012919611

Balboa Press rev. date: 08/11/2014

Contents

Acknowledgements

~

Thank you, my love, for being who you are. To my beautiful children, Jonathan, Anthony and Karina, you guys make me who I am today. I am grateful and humbled by your unconditional love. The encouragement and acceptance I have received has been a blessing in my life. When I need to learn, I will turn to my loved ones. Thank you, and God bless you.

To Balboa Press, thank you for the opportunity to publish what was in my heart.

To Dr. Wayne W. Dyer, thank you for igniting the spark.

"For every one that asketh receiveth; and he that seeketh findeth; and to him that knocketh it shall be opened."

– Jesus –

Introduction

~

It's been eight years since that fateful night. A spark was ignited in me at a time in my life when I needed answers. It came from, of all places, a Public Broadcasting Service program hosted by the one and only Dr. Wayne W. Dyer. Some would call what happened to me an *awakening*, and I guess I would have to agree. Heck, I was in a state of blissfulness for three weeks soon after that night. People close to me saw and understood that something transformative was happening. Others thought I had gone mad.

Prior to all of this, I was just another guy, married to a beautiful woman who loved me very much, with three incredible, God-sent children. I worked at a job that paid the bills, and I socialized here, there and everywhere with family and friends. Privately, though, I was struggling with how I was as a person, a husband and a father. I knew deep down that things had to change with me. I wanted to change. I wanted to be a better person, a happier and calmer human being. I was a good guy, but I wasn't always living that way. And those pesky little bad habits that aren't healthy for a person kept intruding, preventing me from reaching a state of peace.

I was thirty-five when I realized there had to be more to life than this daily grind of *work, party, sleep and work some more.* Everything around me seemed to blend into the next—living the same old thing, over and over and over. I wasn't just going through the motions of life, work and family; I was unsettled, unhappy and frustrated, all at the same time. I certainly had no reason to be, as I was healthy, and I had a roof over my head, food on the table and a family who loved and supported me. And yet, living this way was not enough anymore. Something was creating inner turmoil to a point where my children were starting to witness too much. I was becoming more and more unsettled. My crankiness reached a level that even I did not understand—not to mention the impact it had on the household.

I knew work was not going to change, and I loved my family very much, but something was amiss, and things were starting to burst at the seams—especially concerning my emotional state of mind. So, I privately asked for HELP—literally and figuratively. Who was I asking? I guess as a person of faith I was asking God or any other powerful being to help me get out of this rut. Life wasn't fun anymore. It was mundane, hard work, too much responsibility, stressful, complicated, demanding, fast paced, mean, aggressive at times and relentless in its requirements of me.

Then one evening, as though someone had decided to have fun with me, I landed on a Public Broadcasting Service (PBS) channel where some guy was yacking about life and our purpose in it. At the time, I had no idea who this person was, but his spiel was making a lot of sense to me. For those of you who don't know about Dr. Dyer, he has written many self-help books on life and spirituality—to me, he is a spiritual teacher and "Ascended Master," if you will.

Anyway, I was transfixed. Every word Dr. Dyer said seemed to give me an increased feeling of hope and understanding. It was as though he was specifically talking to me about my issues and concerns. I'm not sure how my wife felt about me, as I ignored most of the family while watching this broadcast about life. I suppose she heard bits and pieces of the telecast and realized this was something I needed to hear, and so I was left to listen without much interruption. It was the most important thing that could have happened to me at that time. This guy, Dr. Wayne W. Dyer, knew what he was talking about, and I was definitely going to follow up on some of his books he'd written. I needed to learn more.

It dawned on me at that moment that it was possible my requests and prayers for help were finally being answered, and I was not about to question anything that crossed my path. By the time the show was done, it sure felt like I was on my way to getting some direction on how to improve my situation. There are not enough words to explain the importance of that chance encounter with Dr. Dyer, which quite specifically catapulted me on a new path of discovery. At that moment, I knew that although there was work to be done to improve the way I was thinking and reacting to life, I now had direction and specific instructions on how to change things around me. Thus began my journey.

I ordered a package from the show, which included one of Dr. Dyer's numerous books (*Getting in the Gap: Making Conscious Contact with God through Meditation*) and a meditation-type manual with a CD to help me get started. By the time my order arrived, I was fired up and ready. I even remember making a promise to myself that this new path and journey I was embarking on was one thing I would see all the way through. No way would I turn back to the old path. It was threatening my marriage and hurting my children. That would not work for me anymore. "Bring on the new path. I'm ready."

I have never had the amount of conviction and determination about anything in my life as I have with this journey of discovery. Whatever has caused me to be so steadfast with the decision to change, I am grateful for it. For seven years, I read self-help, motivational and inspirational books. During this time, I questioned, contemplated, studied, listened to CDs, meditated, observed, practiced, learned and prayed. Finally, I came to the conclusion that it was time. I was ready, no matter the outcome. It was time to release all I had learned since my journey of getting to know me began. From the ages of thirty-five to forty-two, I learned many lessons, and I'm still learning.

Fortunately, during this time, Twitter came along, and creating my Twitter account triggered me to start writing, to become a "wanna be" author. I wrote eleven tweets, which essentially became the titles for each chapter in this book. Go figure. In fact, when I wrote the eleventh tweet, I knew I was finished with that kind of writing and that these tweets had to become part of a book.

If, whoever you are, you are reading this book right now, then know I have made it. I have made it to a place of relative clarity, humility and peacefulness. My wish is that these words I share with you today will help you in your journey of discovery.

Enclosed in this book are truths and beliefs that are found in every human being. May your process of evolving to a higher state—to a better you, the true leader, the true warrior, the real you, the happier you, the peaceful you—begin.

I used to have a hard time saying "God bless," but today, I wish you only happiness, health, peace, love and joy. May God, the source, pure energy or whatever form you wish to call it, bless you for eternity.

Love Always,

Tony Bosnjak

"Darkness cannot drive out darkness; only light can do that. Hate cannot drive out hate; only love can do that."

Dr. Martin Luther King, Jr.

Chapter 1

Positivity is the *Only* Way Out of Negativity

I conducted an experiment with some friends and co-workers, based on positivity and the notion that many people lack positivity in their lives. The experiment was definitely rudimentary; however, the outcome proved to be an eye-opener for those engaged in the challenge. The idea was simple, and if you so choose, I encourage you to conduct a similar experiment with yourself, family, friends and/or co-workers.

Here's how it works. For the next few hours—and, if you're so inclined, the next few days—be only positive. Think only positive thoughts, say only positive things, do only positive acts and expose yourself only to positivity. Now, unless you are an extremely positive person, the exercise is (and was for us) harder than anticipated. It showed me and others how much of the time our society is bombarded by negativity. It also made us realize that our perceptions of things include negativity on a regular basis.

People are generally very habitual. Without knowing it, many, including myself, have negative thoughts and use negative phrases or words in their conversations. For some reason, many of us have made it a habit to be negative—so much so that, when asked, "How are you doing?" we go into some long-winded explanation about all our issues and pains: "I have a headache...I didn't sleep very well last night...I have no money...I'm bored," and on and on and on.

Believe it or not, those simple but very powerful negative responses start to cling to you like a bad habit. No matter what situation you're in, you find yourself always communicating in this manner. This negative habit is not life-ending, but from experience I can assure you that if you continue, a grey cloud of misery soon hovers over you like an endless cold, rainy season. And not realizing it's the negativity bringing you down, you resign yourself to these depressed feelings: "That's just the way it is." You are drained of energy, and your health takes a beating as a result.

Years can fly by. This subtle act of seeing things negatively, or having negative thoughts about others, or making negative comments pulls you into a pit of illusions. Nothing is truly real in this state of negativity. It takes hold of many people's perceptions about things and twists the truth into something that is not real. You essentially become a hostage to it but don't realize the drawbacks. To you, it might even feel as though you're being creative and constructive in your negative ways. Maybe you justify your negative approach to life by making the argument that there are two sides to a coin, and you're just expressing the other side.

And this is exactly how negativity quietly takes control of who you are.

Time as you know it passes, like an empty train on a track that leads to nowhere. The habit of being negative festers in your mind, causing frown lines that become deeper and deeper. Eventually, you start to realize that something isn't right. You're tired of feeling down and disconnected. You hate the fact that you're always pessimistic. By this point, you may even have seen a doctor to help you with your moods, depression and attitude. In some cases, this is necessary, and professionals are needed to diagnose and treat certain disorders. However, for many of us, it can be as simple as acknowledging the need to change certain self-taught behaviours. Cognitive therapy (which involves modifying beliefs, changing behaviours and relating to others in different ways) is a relatively new approach that some doctors are now using in conjunction with other traditional treatment methods.

But many people try to cope through "mood enhancers," be those prescription pills, alcohol or drugs. Unfortunately, these have side effects, leaving their users with even more to manage. You realize that nothing has changed, things still suck and you don't know what is to blame for that horrible feeling.

You try to lose yourself in TV, which might give you some temporary relief from life's demands. On one channel, you have a recap of the day's news. The dollar is down, fewer jobs are being created, a war in the eastern hemisphere rumbles on, drought continues elsewhere, etc. Change the channel and now you get the wonderful opportunity to watch other people's misery and drama. At first it's funny, but like the negative habits I've mentioned, the energy from this show quickly clings to you. Finally, it's time for bed. What a day! But at last, sleep and a break from the day's events. Is it really a break though? Are your last thoughts before sleep about good things, or are they a review of all the crap that went on that day?

The next day at work, you go for coffee with co-workers and discuss yesterday's events. Or maybe you're not at work but visiting a friend, and you both get into details about the juiciest gossip you know. This becomes routine and is, in your mind, relatively harmless, but you're still that unsettled, cranky person. And why not? Years of practice have allowed us to perfect the art of faultlessly thinking and/or talking about others or issues in a negative light.

This all might sound a bit extreme, and I do understand that many of us live our lives quite happily, despite there being negative days. For me, though, it is important to stress here that our slight and subtle negative ways do add up for *some* people. Negativity may even compound other issues a person is dealing with. So for those people who do struggle with this clingy habit or for those who want to improve who they are, let me try to put the consequences of being negative in another way. Judgement of others most certainly rests heavily on one's heart. The energy of judging is clearly rooted in darkness, and you will not know the difference until you practice positivity.

Judging through your thoughts or by talking negatively about a person or situation does not happen as a fleeting moment with no consequences whatsoever. One must realize that those "justified" negative subtle expressions, whether made privately in your own mind or expressed verbally to others, are like poison-tipped daggers. Negativity not only harms the person you are attacking—it also releases, with much greater potency, its venom back on the perpetrator. And if you're not sure what this looks like, take a moment to reflect back on those times when you were not the most positive person to be around, and recall how you felt.

The act of being positive, even when you must force it, is an act of kindness towards yourself. Being positive has nothing to do with others. It is all about you, the most important person in the world.

Remember that age-old expression "If looks could kill..."? Usually, it applies to someone having a "bad" thought about the person the look is intended for. This is precisely when one (the person giving the look) should take a quiet moment to release the negativity/venom. This step is crucial for moving on to the most important step of living in positivity: namely, replacing these mean thoughts with a positive thought directed at that person or thing. You will be amazed at how positivity changes your entire perception about a person or thing. Believe me, sending energy, good or bad, to someone is very real. And know that this energy is always returned—call it karma, if you will.

How many times in a day do we beat people up with negativity...people we know, people we call friends, neighbours, co-workers and family? We thrash them about, crucifying and condemning them in our private thoughts because of our perceptions of who they are or what they've done. "What a b-tch Sally is; she thinks she's so smart," or, "Oh that John, he's such a cocky jerk." Misguided thoughts, and for what? Maybe Sally really is smart and John really does know his stuff.

We've got to stop this insidious habit. It may feel harmless, justified and rewarding, but it's not. Take the time for positive thoughts about those you may have mentally attacked in the past. Create a positive reason in your mind as to why so-and-so never says hi to you. You will be amazed at the effects this has on the person you are sending good energy to, albeit subconsciously. It's as though their bodies feel the "good vibes" and adjust to how you now feel: positive. You'll both win—I guarantee it.

You become healthier and stronger by the simple act of viewing things in a positive light. There is no debate about this. Be positive and find out for yourself. Positivity allows you to expand your own healing capabilities to others. Positivity will soon make you realize how inaccurate negative-based perceptions of others really are. It is your mind and those darn assumptions we make about others that throw you off track. I am 100 percent confident in saying that negativity misguides us in our judgements and perceptions. It closes us off from *all healthy* relationships.

Take these words and hear me NOW!

Positivity is the *only* way out of negativity.

Feeling down? OK, go stand in front of a mirror every morning and tell yourself, "I love you," ten times. Joy comes smashing through every time. Even for the macho guy.

The minute you catch yourself being negative, stop. I give you permission to stop from joining in on negative conversations, even if they're among friends. Choose positivity and see where the conversation takes *you*. Remind yourself that you are a good person and that there is no need to talk badly. Remember, negativity will bring you down and make you sick physically, emotionally and mentally. If the mood among friends does not allow for positivity then politely excuse yourself so that you do not become entangled in negativity, which can affect your entire day. Now, I understand that in some situations, it's impossible to get away. These moments are crucial, as they can pull you back, albeit temporarily, into a world of undue harm. So stay quiet, calm, cool and collected, and if necessary, visualize a white bubble around you to protect yourself from negative attachments.

The more you practice, the more the power of positivity will exude through your pores and permeate your whole being. Over time, you will be able to shift your mind from a negative state to a positive state at will. This ability allows you to take full control of your day and how you move through it. You stop noticing the grey, cloudy days. Your inner being becomes more positive. As a result, your day-to-day duties and encounters are met with a positive mind frame. This state of mind changes how you perceive things. All of a sudden, life is starting to become easier and lighter. Negativity repulses you, and you finally realize how powerful positive thinking really is.

Now you have an understanding about the impact negative words and thoughts can have on your life, and you don't dare attempt those waters ever again. You see other people engaging in negativity, but you don't jump into the fray, unless perhaps to add a positive spin on the topic of discussion. People around you and who know you start to appreciate the energy you give off. Soon you are teaching them what you have learned, whether through your words or your actions.

Living a life in which your mind is focused on positivity

creates a world of simplicity. Problems—or what you viewed as problems—become less of an issue, both in your mind and in your reality. This occurs because your attention is placed on the positive outcome. All your energy is redirected towards being and living positively, an act and strategy that will never harm you but only uplift you.

A negative, fearful and stressful response to anything is harmful and useless. This reaction only perpetuates and gives power to the perceived problem. I use the word "perceived" because there are two ways of perceiving: with a negative mind or a positive one. A negative mind sees only problems. Generally, every problem or thing you need to take care of, if dealt with in a negative mind state, causes stress, anxiety, panic and, finally, health-related issues.

Please start applying positive thinking to anything and everything. Learn to see the world and life as a beautiful gift with nothing in it to fear or dread. This is how it should be and is. Remind yourself, "It will be okay. I can do this. I am not afraid. I've been through harder things in my life and made it. I am a survivor. It will work out. God is with me. I am not alone. I am a good person. The human race is good, and love is real..."

Just try it. Trust me.

"Sitting in meditation is a life-line to your center, to the earth. By calming the mind, you can re-align with your essence."

Dr. Judith Orloff

Chapter 2

Meditate

Meditation was the first step I took, the first lesson I was to learn and the first technique I utilized in achieving peace of mind and balance in my life. This was what I needed to move on, forward and up. I had no idea how important meditation would become and the contribution it would make to my improvement as a human being.

I started out by studying and using the method described in one of Dr. Dyer's books on meditation. He gave clear instructions about the meditative process and the method to use.

It's simple. Recite the first line in the Lord's Prayer: "Our Father who art in heaven, hallowed be Thy name." Eyes closed, visualize each word, and each letter in each word, while slowly breathing in and out. Start with the first word, "Our," seeing the word in your mind's eye. Break the word down by visualizing each letter in that word—first "O," then "u" and finally "r." Absorb the word and each letter. Do not be distracted by other thoughts, which most likely will enter your mind. Slowly and peacefully release those thoughts and simply return to the visualization of the word and its letters. Now move to the next word, "Father," and repeat the process, visualizing the word and then the individual letters comprising the word. Between the words *Our* and *Father* is a gap, which is where you eventually want to rest prior to moving onto the next word. Repeat the visualization process for each word, letter and gap until the entire sentence is complete. You may pause in the space between the words for as long as you like, listening to your breath—inhaling and exhaling. Of course, you need to find a quiet space where you will not be disturbed. Also, please note that my explanation here is a very short and simplified version of the book I read. There are many other books and techniques you can use to help you, too.

I have fallen in love with meditation. Over the years, I've tried other forms, such as concentrating on a flickering candle flame, as well as listening to meditation music. All are fabulous techniques, and to benefit fully from meditation, you must find what works for you. At the end of the day, the goal is to have peace of mind through relaxation and through conscious contact with your higher self.

Unfortunately, it is too difficult to express with words what meditation does for a person. It's something you just have to experience for yourself. It takes time and commitment, but the rewards are life changing. I really do believe that meditation can lead most people to a place of calm, clarity and peace.

Since this chapter is on meditation and how important it has been in my life, I will attempt to write about it in a way that I very much hope will entice you into trying it. Meditation has proven, in my experience, that it can transform how you are as a person.

I travel to the island of Maui, Hawaii, as much as I can. It is such a calm and peaceful place. On one of my visits, while strolling along Kaanapali Beach, I spotted a person receiving a soothing massage from a professional masseuse at one of the local resorts. I sat there for a moment, completely in awe of how incredibly relaxing the massage looked—and simultaneously taking into consideration where I was, as well as hearing the beautiful sounds of the ocean. The scene was so pleasant and peaceful.

Now imagine starting every day in this manner, with a one-hour, ocean-side massage on one of the most beautiful beaches in the world. At first, you might think this is too good to be true, but the longer you lie there, falling deeper and deeper into pure bliss, the more content you become. Images and thoughts of love, peace and joy wash over you like the ocean on the white, sandy beaches of Kaanapali. You don't want this relaxed, happy feeling to end.

Unfortunately, your hour is up, and you must leave for work. It's okay, though. You feel on top of the world, like nothing can stop you, refreshed and ready to go. Every part of your body is booming with peace, calm and an unimaginable sense of strength and power. While driving to work, you reflect on the massage and the feeling you have. You're almost in disbelief at how good you feel from a single massage. You take a breath in and appreciate the moment. Then all of a sudden, you hit traffic. Now you're late for work. You have a deadline to meet, and the pressure is back on. The boss is moody, co-workers are crabby and there are still eight hours of work to go. At the end of the day, you're back on the highway. Unfortunately, there's an accident up ahead, and now for sure you won't be home until 7pm. So, you let your imagination take over. You go back to that place early in the morning when all you had to deal with was a soothing massage. Oh, how wonderful it was. If only you could be there now. What you would do for just ten more minutes of that tranquility. Screw it; you decide that once you get home, you're booking another ocean-side massage for that evening. It's perfect: the masseuse has an opening at 7:30pm, an ideal time, as this is when the sun starts to set on the day, and there's nothing like a sunset in Maui.

The hour massage comes and goes but so has all the drama, worry and stress of that day. You know work is waiting for you tomorrow, but the relaxed, happy and confident state of mind causes you to fear nothing. Your sleep that night is like no other you have had before, so deep and still. The next day is born, and you realize you get to start your day with another ocean-side massage. You're even more excited today than you were yesterday. You realize how important it is for you to start the day with a clear mind, knowing your sanity is at stake. You give thanks and blessings to this all-important massage.

The world, work and traffic await you, but first you tend to your needs. Off to the masseuse you go. Only positive images, sounds and thoughts enter your mind. Once again, you become relaxed, calm, peaceful, confident and rejuvenated. The hour is up, but today is slightly different. The traffic does not bother you as much. The boss might be stressed, but for some reason that does not affect you. It's as though you have a force field on. Work is demanding, but you realize that you can do only what is humanly possible. You laugh a little more, you're more positive, things aren't as troubling and soon you're back on the road, booking another appointment for that ocean-side massage.

Does this give you a better sense of what meditation could do for you?

Meditation is not only a means to an end (peace), it is a *necessary* technique. It gives you a break from all the crap that goes on in your mind. It does even more than this, but I will explain those details shortly. For now, simply know that meditation can refocus you onto higher thought habits. What I mean is this: when we pause, listen and watch our daily thoughts and actions, we realize how much time we spend worrying and living in fear and stress. The ego will fool you into believing you must worry about everything because that's just the way it is. Wrong—and meditation will prove the ego wrong. It does take practice, but over time, the ego, which tries to keep you in the world of fear, is muted during your meditation. This muting of the ego is a key factor to raising your own thought patterns and energy levels. The raising of your consciousness to a higher state during meditation occurs because we never normally take the time to quiet our ego. Regular meditation prevents the ego from dominating your day. It does take practice, but during these quiet periods, the natural state of the mind remembers and desires to go back to the way it is— free of fear, worry, anxiety and stress. Meditation will reintroduce your mind to that desired way of being, an experience you will soon enjoy your entire life.

Meditation, when done regularly, is no different than that daily massage, except here we massage the mind. Meditating will help stop the mind from racing around. A secondary benefit, of course, is that the body indirectly receives a calming and relaxing metaphorical massage. Anxious, fearful, depressed and stressed out people will see incredible benefits.

Meditation has done all these wonderful things for me and much, much more. My meditation times have evolved for me. I continue to receive all the same benefits others do. However, it is also a time when I connect to my higher self and God. I try to live at this level twenty-four hours a day, but if I slip, meditation once again reconnects me to who I really am.

Just for a moment, close your eyes and sit quietly, imagining all the good things about you. Feel the love for yourself and for humanity. Embrace that moment and hold it dear to your heart. Expand your thought now to an even more incredible you, a giver of life, love and joy, a powerful being who only wants peace, joy and love for all. Now share this wonderful light located in you with the rest of the world, one person at a time. In every encounter, know that the beautiful light inside you is extending outward to that person or those people, showering them with a feeling of joy they have never felt before. Privately bless the person you are walking by with an intensity of love so strong it could only come from divinity. That is who you are, and if you don't believe me, meditate on it.

I still practice meditation, and even though it's been several years, as I sit and prepare for a session, I'm constantly reminded as to why I started and always grateful that I continue the practice.

If I still have not convinced you of the benefits, please allow me one last time to show you how it has changed my life. I am able to find and be in peace when I meditate. All the crazy stuff that goes on in life and in the world disappears. Whether it is for fifteen, twenty, thirty or sixty minutes a day, I have complete peace of mind. A bonus feature during this period is that my mental and physical batteries become recharged. As I come out of my meditative state, I am blessed further. My waking and sleeping hours are met with a smile and the calm only an ocean-side massage could attempt to mimic.

People often say that when you are engrossed with a project for work or school, but you feel stuck or maybe have writer's block, you should step away from the project for a short period of time, remove yourself so you can gain a different or better perspective when you return to it. Smart advice, and this is exactly what daily meditation does for the body, mind and soul.

Maybe you just quarreled with your partner, and things are really getting nasty, so you both decide you need a time out. Usually when you return, you've forgotten what you were fighting about—another fine analogy of what meditation is and does. It seems to wipe the worry, angry and fearful slate clean.

I have personally been able to control and release old anxiety habits. So many mental doors have been opened and ah-ha moments have occurred during meditation. There is no other way to explain it than to just say DO IT! Find a technique that resonates with you and don't stop. I can guarantee you will experience all the benefits mentioned in literature about meditation—from feeling younger to looking younger to being rejuvenated and more peaceful.

For those of you who currently don't meditate, I'm sure you

can appreciate sitting quietly by yourself, not being bothered by anyone (including your wonderful kids) for twenty minutes a day, every day. Surely this would have a significant impact on your health; how could it not? Our minds race around way too much not to need some reprieve from the day-to-day grind. Give yourself that gift so you may return the favour to those still racing around in their minds. It's something we all desperately need and will benefit from. Thank you.

"Live a good, clean life. Have a healthy diet, get exercise, don't use alcohol or drugs—or at least do the best you can."

Tony Bosnjak

Chapter 3

Break on Through to the Other Side

This entire book is about personal reflections and lessons I've learned throughout my life, especially in the last seven to eight years. But the information contained in this particular chapter is one of the key factors I needed to face head on, to break on through to the other side.

Consumption of alcohol and drugs is the root cause of standing still and, for some, the cause of moving backwards. I believe these substances are why many of us are not able to advance. The desire to evolve to a higher level is very present in each and every one of us, but to actually attempt to move to a higher level—a higher consciousness, if you will—while under the influence of alcohol or another drug is virtually impossible, in my opinion.

Will casual drinking prevent you from achieving or advancing? Not necessarily, but I'm not talking about having a drink or two once in a blue moon. Those of you who know what

I'm talking about here understand that it's not the amount you consume (although this is something to consider as well). It's who you become when you consume. Personality changes don't just happen in those moments of consuming alcohol or drugs. This stuff changes you and keeps you in that altered personality state twenty-four hours a day, 365 days a year. The impact of these products lasts longer than just the night of partying. Not only do you have to deal with the hangover period, or things you may have regrettably done the night before; alcohol and drugs also change how you behave in the long term. You are never truly the real you when you use these substances.

I am definitely not a biologist, nor do I claim to be an expert on the physiological changes the body goes through when under the influence of alcohol or drugs. However, from what I have personally experienced, witnessed and understood to be true, the natural states of the body and mind are altered. Is this permanent? No, of course not.

Attempting to achieve a balanced state of being, with intermittent breaks between consumption, does not help. The body and mind need prolonged recuperation time. How much time do you give yourself to recoup? What if your goal is to be better than you used to be? Does taking breaks in between party binges make a difference? Are you back to being sweet and kind and relaxed and positive and peaceful when you aren't drunk or high? Maybe you're sweet and kind and funny when drunk. If so, how long do these moments last? Can you go two, three, four months at a time being Mr. or Ms. Wonderful? These are all questions I had to ask myself, and if I didn't like the answer to any of the questions, I knew it was time to look at what was causing me to act so erratically. And usually, for those in the bowels of "consumption and addiction", we see clearly, based on our moods and actions, exactly what needs to be done.

At first, it was hard to accept that things needed to change. Being a weekend partaker was fun. It was the only thing I had to look forward to, actually. What else do you do on weekends and days off?

A weekend alcoholic generally only has four or five days in between to reduce any of the toxic effects of partying with drugs or alcohol. Over the years, this consumption accumulates—not only physically, but mentally and spiritually. Sure, you might slow down a bit as you age or because circumstances change, like marriage, children, new career and so on, but by this point, the mind craves the consumption, keeping you in standby mode instead of take-off mode. I think this is why so many of us keep wondering whether there is more to life than just this.

How many times can we not wait for the weekend? "I just want to unwind." Maybe you go out with friends or stay home and pound a few back. Maybe as a parent you are better disciplined, so you control the frequency or the amount of consumption. Instead of every weekend, it's once a month, and instead of twelve beers, it's six. Or maybe instead of several joints a month, it's only a couple. This is definitely progress—but I'm talking here about breaking through to the other side. Oh, and how sweet it is.

If you start to question your lifestyle regarding booze or pot (and I use these just as two examples of the many that are available), then question away. You certainly don't have to be afraid of reflecting on whether or not you consume too much, especially if those substances change who you are. My personality changed, and I did not like the things I did when under the influence. I was not very nice to my family or to myself. It was difficult for me to be a peaceful person, as my body chemistry changed when consuming. It took me a long time to realize that consumption of these products was a big reason for my personality defects. Maybe booze and pot weren't the only factors, but I can assure you that with those items out of the equation, the answers to some of my life questions came more easily—hence, this book.

This realization did not come out of the blue. I quit all that shit for a good three years. It was only then, during this break, that I saw who I was and who I wanted to be. I could see clearly how these external chemicals I was putting into my body really did change me.

In those three years, I became more relaxed. I tolerated much more and was patient with myself and others more than I could ever have imagined. My anger dissipated. For the first time in a long time, I knew I was not weak. A window had opened, showing me very quickly who I really was. I was strong, healthy, loving, patient, in control and happy.

Then I convinced myself I could partake again—just a little bit.

Thank God for those three years of clarity. The memory of those life-altering years stayed with me, and I soon refocused. I like sobriety. I just had to embrace it, make it part of who I am, and do the best I could with it. And that's exactly what I'm doing to this day.

I can understand why so many people have a hard time seeing life without "partying." From the ages of fourteen to about thirty-four, which is a good twenty years, I was in party mode. This seemed okay, as everyone else around me was also in party mode. Nothing too major at first, and really nothing too major throughout those years, I guess. I definitely wasn't drinking every day, and the drug scene only really happened during my university years. Hell, most of us went through this phase. It's only once you have a bit more responsibility in your life that you realize, "I can't party as hard as I used to," which is a good thing. And thankfully, most of us take those responsibilities seriously. Again, I don't want to make it sound as though having fun in a certain way is bad. When it changes you, though, then it might be something to look at. Simply put: If your partying ways bring negativity into your life, then it's time to question what you are doing.

That being said, there seems to be a shift going on among current young people and some of us older farts. People are realizing that there is a cooler way to go through life. In fact, I'm starting to believe that the old days of partying with copious amounts of booze or drugs are passé. When I see other people who live a clean life, I realize how far we have come as a society, and I'm starting to see more and more people living more cleanly.

As someone who is trying his best to live a good, clean life, I can tell you that there is so much more out there to touch, taste, smell and do when you're clean and sober. It's as if more doors begin to open. You're not afraid to try new things. You decide you want more for yourself. Hell, why not eat more healthily, too? You begin to desire better for yourself and for others. It is only natural for you then to experience a burning desire to go beyond what you pictured yourself to be. The mind is clear, the body is healthy and before you know it, circumstances in your life lead you to a place greater than you had thought possible.

Years pass, and when you look back on all that has been

accomplished, you are grateful for that one strong, determined decision to still have fun but to move through life with clarity. Those who can appreciate the mountains you have climbed to get where you are today embrace you and love you.

You know you don't need chemicals to have a good time. Purity of body, mind and soul becomes your new addiction, and this new addiction is not a scary one to face. I've slipped, but that craving for pureness, clarity of mind and calmness in life is too strong to ignore or to stop trying for. A no-fear attitude remains with you, as you reach higher and higher states of being. The pull is too strong, and the end result is unavoidable. Success is your only outcome, but you must take that first step and make the only strong, determined decision—to have fun differently.

You're not alone. In fact, there are more of us than you think who have made the decision, and even more who want to live that new, exhilarating, adventurous, fun and healthy lifestyle.

The following is an excerpt from my oldest boy's high school project about "Healthy Living", created when he was fourteen. He made a collage, and these were his thoughts.

> The picture of the beer, cigarette and marijuana leaf represent me having an alcohol, drug and smoke free life. It's important for me to live a life free of these addictions for lots of reasons. I don't want to ruin my life and the people close to me. I decided it's not the path I want to take. My other reason is because I'm looking to have a bright future in hockey and make it to a high level. By

not falling within the grasp of these chemicals it makes it that much easier to accomplish that goal.

The cost of living an addiction free life is absolutely Zero. The steps to living this clean life involve me having a strong mind and soul and being able to say NO. I've been around people, friends and family that have fallen down the wrong path. When they learned from their mistakes they were able to guide me and tell me—Jonny, don't make the same decision I made, you'll think it's a fun life to be intoxicated until you find out how much more fun it is to live a clean life. In the end it's your decision, it's easy to say yes but it's just as easy to say no to this stuff. I chose no.

Observe a child and how he or she plays and moves through life. Children truly do live purely, and they have an amazing time enjoying life. This is how I want to live my life. If they can do it, why can't I or you? It's no longer acceptable or fair to tell our young ones, "Do as I say, not as I do."

"I am only one, but still I am one. I cannot do everything, but still I can do something. I will not refuse to do the something I can do."

Helen Keller

Chapter 4

Always Have Faith, No Matter What

Always have faith, no matter what. Soon, the sun's rays will shine upon you. But until then, prepare yourself. Some work is required.

Having faith means a whole lot of different things to a whole lot of people. I like to equate it to having hope. This doesn't mean you should sit idle, though, hoping that things will get better and life will be fantastic.

Somewhere along my journey, I remember hearing that we must at least meet God halfway, and he will then do the rest for us. This is essentially what the present chapter is about. Some work is required to reach the "promised land". Everybody wants to have a great life, and I know that this is possible. Having faith simply means that you are aware that all your good efforts at being a good person and living a good life do not go unnoticed. God, the angels, all the ascended masters and every soul in heaven—all want only happiness and peace for each of us.

As we live on Earth, we have many challenges, some of us more than others. I feel as though my life is somewhat of a training ground for the next beautiful and incredible life I will have—a reincarnation to the next level, based on my efforts and current lifestyle.

Say, for example, you live from a selfish standpoint. Everything you do and say has to be about you. Well, life will then give you lessons on selfishness. Meaning, the more selfish you are, the more experiences you will encounter in your life where a choice can be made to be either selfish or unselfish. These scenarios repeat themselves over and over until you choose to be selfless, experiencing what that must feel like. These lessons are very important to advance closer to a state of enlightenment.

Or say you're the type of person who steals from others. You will continue to be in situations where you have the choice to steal or not to steal. The choices you make will have consequences. When you stop stealing and learn the lesson, you will be rewarded in life—and this is what faith is all about. It's knowing that doing and living the right way, as opposed to, say, stealing, will lead to better things (love and peace).

The level at which *you* live life is different from that of any other human being. Some find themselves less fortunate, living a life of homelessness. There are others who live a life full of wealth and prosperity. Yet, the goal for all lives remains the same. The challenges are different, but the opportunities and choices to advance as a human being are the same. It does not matter what your starting point is; what matters are your choices. Having faith that right action and right choices will lead you to the "promised land" (peace and contentment) is a major ingredient in finding your way.

And so, it is no surprise that so many of us believe in a higher power. All across the earth—from tribes, to nomads, to first-world civilizations—we worship God or gods. We have faith in something that we don't actually see, touch, smell, taste or hear, yet we hold onto the notion that there is something out there greater than us, something that urges us to live our lives to our fullest potential. Each individual has his or her own path; but the ability to move into a place where true love and peace reside is accessible to each and every one of us.

Why is there a belief in a higher power or energy that is beautiful, helpful and all-loving? From the beginning of time, people have believed in a higher source. We have turned to this source countless times. From kings to presidents to well-known saints like Mother Theresa, all have turned to this higher power for guidance and help.

And why not?

You either believe in a God or gods or a higher source or you don't. You either want to live in a loving way with peace in your heart or you don't. I am not here to convince you of this presence. I am here to encourage you to use God, the angels, all the saints and any other source or energy you feel can help you in your life when needed. Throughout my life, I have used that higher source to my advantage and got myself out of some sticky situations. Quite frankly, God or Jesus or the archangels or whatever source you call upon for help is very excited to be there for you. Helping is their joy.

In some ways, I guess I was lucky that my parents forced me to go to church when I was very young. Church introduced me to God, Jesus, Mother Mary, the angels and all the other wonderful characters found in the Holy Bible. And even though I found mass to be very robotic and boring, I must admit the messages, at times, were important. Yes, it was the same old info I'd heard over and over for forty-plus years, but some things did sink in. The only thing I could not understand was how so many people were devoted to Sunday mass. I would go out of obligation or guilt. I guess my faith was weak.

Today, my faith is strong. Not because I go to church every Sunday. I don't. But because I realized faith is in ourselves.

You cannot find or get faith outside of yourself. To possess faith does not require you to belong to an organized religion or to confess your sins over and over. Faith is something we are all born with. It is placed deep down within our souls. It cannot be lost or given away. It is part of your internal guidance mechanism. Faith shows you the way, and the more you believe, the more devotion you will have for God.

When I do go to church, or even when I pray, I now have a better appreciation and understanding of why people attend church or pray regularly. It's about having that strong connection to your source. I truly believe that we cannot live without this. I don't consider myself a religious person, but I do have deep devotion for God. I am not a born-again, Bible-thumping fanatic. This is not necessary. What I'm talking about here is private. It is a relationship between you—and only you—and God, Source, Energy, Wisdom or whatever you choose to call it. It is very personal and should remain that way.

At the "I Can Do It" conference in Vancouver, BC, in 2011, Dr. Dyer introduced us to what I will call the "I AM" concept. That was not the first time it had been introduced to our society, but it was the first time I had heard it. He also discussed a similar concept in greater detail at a workshop I attended in January 2012 on the beautiful island of Maui. It was my understanding that parts of this concept were taken from Exodus 3:14, which describes how God, in the form of a burning bush, spoke to Moses. God revealed to Moses his name: "I AM THAT I AM." This is his name forever.

Without going into great detail, and for fear of not being able to eloquently explain Dr. Dyer's wisdom on who we really are, I strongly recommend you read his book *Wishes Fulfilled—Mastering the Art of Manifesting*. However, so as not to keep you in limbo, this is how I interpret the I AM concept. God specifically uses the words I AM THAT I AM as his name to teach us about who we are. I AM THAT is exactly who you will be; it all depends on what word you use to replace THAT. If you replace the word THAT with the word LOVE, then that is who you are: I AM LOVE. (And by the way, God would never refer to herself as anything not positive. Negativity does not exist in her vocabulary; it can't.)

Based on this information, I realized God and I were one. Now, some might call this blasphemous, but I truly believe this is why God referred to himself as I AM THAT I AM in the story of the burning bush. He quite specifically wanted us to know that we are a part of him, as he is a part of us. I AM will live forever, but how one chooses to see oneself will determine whether one lives one's life using the Lord's name in vain (e.g., I am sick, I am poor, I am weak...) or lives one's life by claiming who one is: "I am strong, I am kind, I am happy, I am love, I am truth, I am optimistic, I am grateful, I am unique, I am beautiful, I am intelligent, I am joyful..." All the things God truly is.

It was during this I AM concept lesson that my faith took hold. I finally understood what it meant to have a strong faith and to be deeply devoted to God. What you're really doing by stating and believing that "I AM LOVE" is showing respect to God and to yourself. God's intention was to show you that you are God as well: His creation, made in his likeness, as himself. And your devotion to God should equal your devotion to yourself and this life you are living.

You might feel as though "yourself" is separate from God, and because of this, you might feel a lack of devotion towards yourself and this life. And you might convince yourself that this lack does not in any way affect your devotion to or relationship with God. But this is not true. You cannot be separate from God. Thus, any lack of devotion towards yourself is a lack of devotion to God. Your ego might try to convince you that you are separate, but remember: ego = fear, anxiety, stress, anger, jealousy, sickness, hatred, misery and negativity—characteristics God does not even recognize. "Yourself" is the I AM, God's name, which = Love, Peace, Joy, Hope, Happiness, Calm, Positivity, Sharing, Caring, Faith. And these are attributes that should be shown deep devotion, as they are a part of you and God.

Move away from what the ego offers and move towards love and peace. When you walk towards love, God not only walks towards you, she brings all of her relatives: confidence, calmness, leadership, guidance, power, truth, compassion, humility, respect, wisdom, graciousness, loyalty, honesty... And the list goes on.

Have faith, and Heaven will be laid at your feet here on Earth.

"I expect to pass through life but once. If, therefore, there be any kindness I can show, or any good thing I can do to any fellow being, let me do it now, for I shall not pass this way again."

William Penn

Chapter 5

It's Easy To Be Mean but Easier To Be Nice

Peace is within you. You were born with it. It's part of your human nature. Peace is who you really are. If you are brave enough to allow peace to be your dominant characteristic, then you will soon realize how easy it is to be nice. Peace is the foundation of kindness. Once you consciously make the decision to be as nice as possible, kindness seems to envelope you. It becomes part of you, like a well-worn coat...as comfortable as any piece of clothing you have ever worn. The more you embrace the effort of being nice to people, the more life and people around you become kind. Kindness is reciprocated.

Deciding you will be nice today creates an energy about you that perpetuates kindness in others. The struggle of always trying to be right or having to prove you are right dissipates. No one really cares if you're right, anyways. People are consumed with their own battles of trying to be right and heard. So what better way to help yourself and others than to be kind?

Kindness produces a drama-free mind. Of course, there are people you know or people you encounter who have not learned this lesson and want drama. They will, inadvertently or not, say things or do things to get under your skin. Smiling and remaining calm and kind defuses any attack those people will launch on your state of mind. Because you are so focused on being kind, the noise these people make is transmuted—sent to God for cleansing.

The important things to remember are that 1) you have made a conscious decision to try your best to be nice and 2) you make every effort to follow through with that decision. I can guarantee you will see immediate results.

We are not a perfect race and, as such, we will inevitably do things that others perceive to be unkind. Similarly, our interpretation of other people's actions may cause us to have negative thoughts about those people or situations. For example, say I'm driving down the street and I get cut off by another driver. "What a jerk!" I shout. "That person doesn't know how to drive! I hate people who don't shoulder check." Now, those are some serious negative comments, and for what? My interpretation of the incident has caused me to judge another, and when judgment is involved, kindness cannot be.

Will I ever really know the true reason why that driver switched lanes when he did? No. And yet, I formed an opinion about the driver: how much of a jerk that person was, and how useless a driver he was. I can't even count how many times I have done this. Unfortunately, we get so consumed with anger and frustration on a daily basis, as in situations like this, and usually over such small things. It makes one realize how little kindness is in our lives. It's possible that the driver did not see us—a simple and innocent mistake. Now, replace your unkind thoughts with nice thoughts for this scenario. "Hey, I'm lucky I saw the driver in front of me change lanes. Drive carefully, sir. I don't want to see you—or anyone else, for that matter—get into an accident." A few kind words, which end the drama and stop you from potentially taking negative thoughts you may have had about that driver and multiplying your frustration onto the next person who is assuredly going to tick you off; thus, the importance of practicing kindness.

I would rather see the snowball effect when someone is in a state of kindness than in a state of anger or, God forbid, rage.

Being a mean person does not come naturally for most of us. We certainly weren't born that way. Usually there is a condition or thought that triggers us to become angry or vengeful. I believe this occurs due to the bad habits we have allowed to fester and grow; at times, we have nurtured them, too. Those bad habits include but are not limited to judging, speculating, making assumptions, gossiping, lying, jealousy, insecurity, selfishness, arrogance, stubbornness, competitiveness, rudeness and conceit. There are others, but I believe these specific ones are key to humanity's inability simply to be nice. Strange, I must say, as these impaired emotions seem to use up more energy and are more time-consuming than simply being kind.

Why, then, does kindness take a back seat to the bad habits? Is it because of the crazy and fast-paced world in which we live? It's as if we must do whatever it takes to have an advantage over others. If that means we trick our mind into believing the lies and judgments we put onto others, then so be it. At least we've convinced ourselves that we are better than others. This makes us feel good. Or does it? Multiply this tactic by six billion people and you get illusions and unreality. The pokes and jabs towards each other become an insidious disease, quietly attacking our natural human state: being nice.

The truth about who you are can become buried beneath all those bad habits, those impaired emotions. Even the little white lies we use to prop ourselves up block any remaining daylight there might be. Now we are defined and viewed by *how* we are instead of *who* we are.

So, it is up to you—and only you—to bring kindness back into your life. This will lift the veil of illusion and expose you to what life is truly about. Your life benefits from this decision to be nice. Even if the ability to be nice remains at a level where nothing mean is said to another, then so be it. This is your starting point. The rest will follow—most importantly, truth. Live your life the way it was meant to be. Our journey on Earth, since the beginning of time, has been to live without illusion. This can only be done when we are kind. Fortunately, our life expectancy is anywhere from eighty-five to ninety-five years. This should give us plenty of time to extinguish our old bad habits with new wonderful habits. But the action starts with you.

Our civilization is guided by the internal consciousness we all carry within us. This is our moral compass. If you want to speed up the process of evolution so that we can immediately recognize the benefits of being nice, then you must start today, living from that place. Waiting for your children to take on that role may not work, as they learn from us. It's that simple.

Check yourself, watch yourself, listen to yourself and observe yourself. By doing this, you engage your true moral compass (niceness). Situations that would have induced anger now will cause you to simply shrug your shoulders and smile politely. This is the correct emotion to have. When this happens, you will find, 100 percent of the time, that the smile was meant for you. Good job. The energy from this new and wonderful reaction is also immediately delivered to anyone else who wants to receive. And trust me, there are a lot of us in need of that energy.

Let's go back to the driving scenario. Instead of reacting in a mean, nasty, angry and frustrated way, you now react positively. You kindly let the person, who is speeding and driving erratically, into the lane. You avoid a confrontation or possibly an accident. The other driver soon recognizes her behavior, corrects herself and appreciates the kind actions on your part. This will give you instant joy, and as you look back through your rear view mirror, you are blessed a second time. The experience and emotions left at the scene are imprinted on your state of mind, and a new way of being is solidified. The realization that you can easily abandon your old, impaired emotions and revert to a peaceful, pleasant experience is life altering. The meaning behind "treat others as you would want to be treated" becomes your ah-ha moment each and every time you show kindness. You can control how *you* behave or react to people or things.

There are times when a strong opinion may be required, but you never have to be mean with your message. It's all in *how* you say things. I'm learning this lesson each and every day with every person I encounter. My family is my greatest teacher.

I am very passionate about the things I am writing in this book, but if there is someone out there who wishes to debate what

I am saying, then I will let them speak their mind. In fact, there might be things I can learn. Having an open mind doesn't mean you are less of a person. This means you are compassionate. Your position on a topic should come from a loving place. Conversely, trying to reason with someone who is in a state of meanness is useless; they can pull you back into the world of illusion. So, remove yourself from judgment and be nice to others.

The book *A Course In Miracles*, published by the Foundation for Inner Peace, contains an incredible description about judging and the world of illusion. The writing will give you a better understanding of how we can trick ourselves into living an illusory life full of attacks and meanness:

> In order to judge anything rightly, one would have to be fully aware of an inconceivably wide range of things; past, present and to come. One would have to recognize in advance all the effects of his judgments on everyone and everything involved in them in any way. And one would have to be certain there is no distortion in his perception, so that his judgment would be wholly fair to everyone on whom it rests now and in the future. Who is in a position to do this? Who except in grandiose fantasies would claim this for himself?

**"It isn't that they can't see the solution.
It is that they can't see the problem."**

G. K. Chesterton

Chapter 6

Let Go and Let God

Every day, there are issues to deal with. Let go of the negative thoughts about an issue and just deal with the issue.

It is a fact that life will always contain issues. Sometimes, these issues may even make you want to scream. No matter who you are or where you live, there is something just around the corner, waiting to bump into you—the thing you must look at head on, that can't be ignored or avoided. It's that issue you knew was coming. Or maybe you were blind-sided by something that you now cringe at the idea of having to deal with. And guess what: when you're done taking care of that business, a new corner approaches.

Life's issues seem relentless, especially when we're adults, dealing with work, children, relationships, family, money, addictions, insecurities, illnesses, friends, enemies, governments, rules, parents, and on and on.

Why do we put ourselves in these predicaments? We don't; that's just the way the world works. Unless you live in a cave on top of a mountain, you are going to encounter all the wonderful things life has to offer, including those "issues" you must deal with. Even our young children must deal with things in life. So, how do we go about handling the various curve balls continuously being thrown our way? In short, the answer is in the first paragraph of this chapter—let go of the negative thoughts about the issue and just deal with it.

Sleep allows us to shut the brain down so we don't think about stuff. Sleep can definitely alleviate, albeit temporarily, the pressure a person might feel about a circumstance that requires attention and a solution. However, sleeping your problems away is temporary. In fact, I truly believe that until you "grab the bull by the horns" and learn how to deal with life's issues, they will forever reside around each corner you take—just to make life more interesting.

Personally, the little issues that constantly expose themselves to me are a pain in the ass. Like you, I've had enough tests and life challenges to last me three life reincarnations. I can't stand them, but I must admit I've learned a ton from those pesky, nagging little issues. I had to. The business I owned with my wife was putting me in a position where I either dealt with the hiccups of running a business in a healthy manner, or I died from a heart attack. Funny thing is, looking back, none of those issues were heart attack worthy. It was my reaction to them that caused my body to respond in a certain way.

Let me clarify by saying that most circumstances/issues outside of our control are not the root cause of our illnesses or ailments, or of our anxiety or fears or other stresses. Don't get me wrong: issues that occur in life are very real and present, not some imaginary problems that will go away by closing your eyes and wishing things were better. Oh no, that would be too easy and not challenging enough. Don't forget, we chose to come to Earth and this life for a reason: to learn and evolve. As such, we accepted the challenge. Therefore, it is important to recognize and remember that most "issues/problems" are not the cause of negative, fearful, anxious or stressed reactions. They are placed in our lives so we can learn. I hope the next few pages help you learn new ways to cope and deal with life's "lessons".

First, reread the title of this chapter, over and over. At least ten times. Second, know that there are issues that you can let go of and let God deal with. Sounds kooky, but there are times in life when nothing you can do will help the situation. Other people's expertise may be required to handle the problem. I learned this the hard way through the operation of my business. The company relies on its equipment to bring in the revenue, so I had to learn quickly that I could not fix all the problems and that I had to trust and rely on others to fix my equipment when it wasn't working. This may sound like common sense to most, but I can assure you that at times when our machinery would break down, it caused me a lot of stress—not because the machine would not get fixed but because of all the other unknown factors I created in my own mind, like when it would be fixed, whether we would get the parts in time, how much it would cost, whether I could trust the repair person, whether customers would complain, whether the machine would work after the repair...and on it would go until the problem was resolved. Sometimes, the frantic thoughts would last for weeks, adding so many additional layers of worry to the mix.

The negative thoughts about an issue that we tend to allow in create a bigger problem (in your mind) than the actual issue at hand. For whatever reason, there are some of us who not only have to deal with whatever it is we need to deal with, but also pack on a layer of worries and negative thoughts about what we are dealing with. Sounds draining, doesn't it? It most certainly is. Not to mention the toll it takes on your body and mind.

What if you permitted your mind to think as positively as possible during these "crisis" type moments—calming thoughts about any situation or "problem" you must deal with? What then? I can tell you, you would probably focus on the issue at hand more quickly. There wouldn't be any fearful or stressed emotions to deal with. You might even enjoy the experience, knowing that a challenge lay ahead, the challenge being, "How can I move through this without having mild heart attacks every time an issue surfaces?" This is the only thing you truly need to focus on. The problem itself will either be resolved or you will move on, letting go and maybe even letting God deal with it. But no one, to my knowledge, has ever been stuck with an issue for eternity. And throughout this whole process of focusing on how you deal with stuff, you might even learn a thing or two along the way. This is exactly what my business partner would always tell me. "Why waste your time and energy worrying about something that hasn't even happened?" She was so right, and I'm truly happy I married her.

It boils down to a mind full of stress and worry or a mind neutral to the task at hand, with a sprinkle of calm and positivity.

You can actually imbue your mind with these attributes. It's your choice. You know it, and I know this to be true. Now, many of my current, just-around-the-corner issues are only issues, not problems that magically produce fearful, stop-in-my-tracks, paralyzing symptoms. The habit of magnifying the issue at hand by adding additional worry-wart scenarios within your mind must stop. All that such negative energy does is make you ill mentally, physically and emotionally.

The journey you must go through when dealing with any issue in life can become either more of a stress than it was meant to be or a journey of observation, wherein you watch the unfolding of the solution as it's happening because you are not consumed with stress, fear or worry—a much happier and more realistic process.

I find that when I get into *solution mode* as fast as possible, thus entirely bypassing the negative mental thought build-up, I become less stressed or anxious about the issue facing me. Getting into solution mode as quickly as possible places your energy into problem solving versus fearful imaginings and thought patterns. This doesn't mean you will receive answers to all things immediately. It simply means you will prevent toxic bad habits from consuming your time. You have a problem you must attend to, and this is exactly what solution mode is for. While in this mode, you can also deal with the rest of life's demands, whether those be children, work, travel, relatives or whatever. The important thing to understand is that when you are in solution mode, no matter how long it takes, you must deal with the problem without fear, stress or anxiety, and *preventing* the negative thoughts about an issue keeps fear, stress and anxiety at bay. Simultaneously, the other parts of your life can be met with peace and calm.

Hopefully, in your decision-making process (solution mode), you have facts you can use to make the process and experience a pleasant one. Going through positive scenarios about the issue that needs resolving is a great mechanism for finding a happy medium. This practice can definitely help you get into solution mode. You must prevent your mind and ego from making life harder for you with their bombardment of scary images and thoughts. This can only be achieved by steadfast determination to deal just with the issue and let all that other garbage fall to the wayside. It is a conscious effort.

This way of thinking will help you move on and forward.

"The reward of a thing well done is to have done it."

Ralph Waldo Emerson

Chapter 7

Pray Always

Dear God, show us how to love ourselves, to love each other and to love Mother Earth. I pray for world peace tonight.

Yes indeed, world peace can be achieved, even if it's one person at a time. Peace must be the core of who you are. Peace and contentment with your life is most important. If there is no peace, you will find turmoil. Praying will help you understand what it is to have peace in your heart. Praying is a link to who you really are. Praying is deep spiritual communication between you and your creator. It must be seen this way and felt in your heart.

The sharing of your thoughts is a pure and natural way of communicating to the divine. This practice should not be taken lightly. Praying is not only a portal to all that is possible and beautiful; it is a lifeline to eternity. The quiet moments you take to talk or ask for guidance are times of great magic and blessings. At these moments, you are one with everything. Peace automatically enters your heart and soul. Pure love radiates from you and to those you pray for. Praying is very powerful, and its full benefits are utilized when you embrace the process of communicating to divine love. Do not offer up empty words or empty actions to God. Prayer must be looked upon as sacred. It is no different from a mother quietly loving her child as they play and roll around. Their deep connection to each other is so simple, yet pure. The power of the mother and child's love for each other is unshakable. The bond between mother and child is unbreakable. Yet in some ways, this serene picture of a loving mother and child joyously playing together pales in comparison with the energy and love that prayer produces.

Prayer is also more than just communication to God, to the angels or to loved ones before bedtime. Praying is a way to live. It is something you can do all day, each and every day. I used to pray before bed, and that would be the end of that. The next day, I would wake up as if nothing had happened; same old guy with the same old problems. Maybe I'd offer up a few words to God during the day, especially when I needed help, but as soon as my prayer was over, I was off to the races or back to my problems. This type of quick prayer, the "get the praying out of the way" approach, is a start. But what I'm trying to convey here is deeper than quick words of prayer to God. The quick words are a part of it all, but what comes *after* praying is just as important. You need to stay loving and close to who you are communicating to at all times— meaning, the process of praying should leave you with a sense of holiness or purity or softness about you that you can share with others. Prayer is a gesture of love, even in times of need, which is sent outwardly to all who encounter you. This is what happens from prayer. This is who you become because of prayer.

I was brought up in a Catholic environment where Sunday church was a must. Prayer every night before bed was also a common practice. Now before I say much more, I have to thank my folks for introducing me to God, Jesus and the Virgin Mary. As simple and easy as it was to say the Lord's Prayer every night like a malfunctioning record player, I must admit, the habit kept me connected to my source. Unfortunately, as I got older, I got sick and tired of going to church. When I moved out on my own, the Sunday trips to church were done. I prayed, but mostly when I needed help. I really never gave God or any other source or energy much time. What was the point? You say a few words, give thanks and nothing happens. Plus, life was moving fast, and I needed to keep up with it. I didn't mind praying, and it's not like I was embarrassed or anything, but I was too busy to take the time to understand what prayer meant. I'm not anymore.

> Dear God, Mother Mary, Jesus and all the archangels. Thank you for everything. Please keep my mind strong and healthy and positive. Protect me and my family as we pass through life, encountering the various lessons we must learn. Please keep the light always shining on me and the rest of the world. Give me strength to face and overcome my fears. Guide me, my wife, my children and the entire world with your love. Help me be open to all the gifts that are sent my way. Dear God, I need your strength. Please remove

any and all negative things from my life. Help me see and hear the wonderful, positive things about life. Help me see and feel myself as you see and know me, as a pure being of goodness, light and love. If there is a place I must be at or a thing I must do, please guide me to where I should be. Your will is my will. Thank you.

Amen

I have had a great life so far, and I've finally learned how wonderful it is to talk with God (Allah, Krishna, Mohammed, Buddha, the source, energy, and saints like Mother Teresa, Mahatma Gandhi and Saint Francis of Assisi). To pray is to feel complete oneness. The beauty of prayer is that it can be about anything. If the words of your prayer are positive, then know that it has been *heard* and *answered*. You must believe this to understand what praying is all about. The power of prayer reaches and extends to every one of us. How? Through your wonderful and kind words. Your desire to be who you really are causes you to become you, the real you, thus impacting our world. There are those who might say praying for yourself is a selfish act, but this is exactly what God wants you to do. He's waiting for your prayers, as he wants his archangels to work. This is their job. This is how the world evolves. This is how new paths are created, how creation itself is born, how peace, love and joy are extended out to yourself and others.

Use what is available to you right now. If you're feeling lost, lonely, scared, depressed, mad, tired, hopeless, frustrated, confused, broken, weary or simply drained, then pray and never stop. Please get into the habit. You don't have to go to church to pray or to have your prayers heard and answered. You just have to pray. Let all your thoughts, dreams, desires and questions be carried to God, and know that she is taking good care of you. Bless yourself and the entire world when you're done praying. Allow yourself to be strong and positive in prayer, as magic happens in this format. Tomorrow and the day after and so forth, repeat the process until the end of time. You will see—you will understand what prayer is for you.

Prayer does not change lives, it creates lives, and it will create the life you are meant to live. From this point on, make prayer a conversation. All your intentions you wish to create for yourself and for the whole world are blessed and brought to fruition when you pray. Through prayer, you have allowed the almighty power to enter and be as it was meant to be. There is no shame in this, as you have become a light for the world to follow. There is strength in prayer, and its strength is offered to you always.

Focus, and with pure intentions say your peace. Do not stop at any cost. You want calm, joy, happiness, success and all the other wonderful things life has to offer? Then stay focused in prayer. This will be your guide, as the heavens above, with all the archangels, Jesus and all other blessed beings, come to help and surround you in light and love.

The world religions definitely have the praying aspect down pat. I will never say anything bad about this practice. Of course, there are times when the traditional practices of a religion might feel mundane and useless, and in fact, these have been some of my opinions about Sunday mass. But as I get older and aspire to be closer to God, to be a better person, less judgmental, I recognize the importance of deep devotion to prayer, and the respect it deserves. Fortunately, this deep devotion and respect is reciprocated. This is the gift prayer gives back. You learn to have deep devotion for yourself and humankind—a win–win situation.

Remember, prayer does not have to take place in a church or temple. It can be done anywhere, even as you walk. The point being, you can place your mind and thoughts on anything at any time in any place.

There's a great book out there by Nawang Khechog, called *Awakening Kindness: Finding Joy Through Compassion for Others.* In it, he talks about walking meditation and offers a saying you can repeat over and over as a form of prayer to awaken kindness: **"May all be kind to each other."**

So, next time you're walking to your car, shopping, strolling through a park or even working, pray a little—everyone benefits.

"Be a Bringer of the Light. For your light can do more than illuminate your own path. Your light can be the light which truly lights the world."

Neale Donald Walsch

Chapter 8

Become a Leader, Not a Follower

To be a leader, you must follow your heart. Your heart is made out of pure Love. All decisions that are based on Love will lead to Joy, Fairness, Equality, Comfort, Relief, Humility, Compassion, Understanding, Patience and so much more. To use only the mind, which has a tendency to overthink, can lead us to fear, hesitation, confusion, uncertainty, competition, anger, jealousy, deception and so on. And because these emotions are not a part of our natural makeup, being contrived by the mind, we then unavoidably make decisions from incorrect data. It's quite easy to see the outcome of decisions based on fear or anger. Pure love is the only source of information on which we should base our decisions.

You might recall the time when the people of Libya were protesting against their government, back in late 2010 and early 2011. At a certain point, it was alleged that the leader had commanded the air force to engage and bomb protesters. On February 21, 2011 it was reported that two fighter pilots of the Libyan army had defected to another country, as they had decided to defy their leaders' orders. In fact, the day they were to shoot innocent civilians, they chose to fly their jets to another country, as their compassion and common sense told them that killing these innocent people was wrong—clearly a decision that most of us can understand and would make quite easily. However, some situations are not so black and white, and as a result, we follow instead of leading the way.

Bullying, for instance, can appear harmless if no physical attack is carried out. We hear all the time that "boys will be boys; they're just goofing around." Today, however, bullying has become a huge topic of discussion. Our schools, along with many parents, have shone the spotlight on bullying, and the more attention we pay to this matter, the less bullying we see. Why? In the past, most of us were too afraid to stand up to bullies. We looked the other way. It's certainly understandable when a child or a group of children are afraid of a particular person. The sheer viciousness of a bully's words and actions can be quite intimidating to most.

Today, it is a different story. Now, we recognize the strength in numbers. But to get to this point, someone had to lead. And based on what I have seen at my own children's schools, teachers and parents alike have finally decided that any kind of bullying, verbal or physical, is 100 percent unacceptable. Unfortunately, it took a ton of stories about children being abused by the physically stronger for society to finally intervene. Over and over, we saw newscasts or written information about a child who had literally been bullied to death. And yes, even though it is sad to say, sometimes these messages needed to come from the afterlife to awaken our hearts to these horrible tragedies. As a result, pure love was entering people's hearts; or rather, I should say pure love was finally being allowed to *lead*. Really, it took those brave children who endured days, months and sometimes even years of bullying to show us the way—by teaching us to open our hearts and lead for what is right.

This lesson has even spilled over into other aspects of our society. There are more and more people who do not accept being pushed around or exploited. The public is demanding more from their governments and big corporations. It's not even that we want more; we just want fairness and equality.

There are, of course, more layers we must peel back to get to the root of why some people still feel they have the right to project their insecurities, anger, fears and greed on others. With all the violence, hardship, crime and wars going on today, our society must approach these issues with an opposite attraction— from a LOVE perspective. Any other approach will only cause defensiveness, uncertainty, confusion and more of the same. A true leader can break this cycle, but copious amounts of courage, faith and love will be needed. Fortunately, we all have a higher power we can turn to for this strength. You just have to be willing to take that step and trust that a loving, compassionate, understanding approach is the right way to go.

We've all heard and read about and maybe even participated in peaceful marches and peaceful protests. Granted, the issues may not have been resolved at that very moment, but the message, along with our actions, spoke volumes. In some cases, the world has been transfixed by the non-violent, peaceful methods people have used to get a point across. Do June 5, 1989, Tiananmen Square and "Tank Man" ring a bell? The incident received worldwide recognition. The day after Chinese government forces violently removed protesters from Tiananmen Square, a lone man, carrying what appeared to be a grocery bag in each hand, put himself directly in front of oncoming Chinese government armoured tanks. The tanks attempted to maneuver around this individual, but each time, the man repositioned himself into the path of the oncoming tanks. The tanks repeatedly tried to reposition themselves, and again this man would step in front of the lead tank. This was truly a tank versus man standoff. In the end, the driver of the lead tank turned off its engines, causing the remaining tank drivers to follow suit.

I ask you: Is there any other way? I'm not suggesting here that if you are attacked in a very physical way, you should not defend yourself or get out of harm's way. But clearly, the message of non-violence this one individual sent to the entire world should put all violent people to shame.

Each and every one of us has at least one strength, one incredible quality about ourselves. That one thing is most certainly needed here on Earth. Through the lessons of pure love, we too can move mountains—or tanks, for that matter. We will leave our mark on humanity, but we must first have the courage to love. True leaders, like Martin Luther King, Mahatma Gandhi and Nelson Mandela, lived from this standpoint. They have proven that love does lead. Not one person, or their strength, is less than another when love is given.

I am grateful that we are all unique. Through our uniqueness, we can teach each other different levels of love. Love and leadership come in all shapes and sizes. But the one thing love does not do is follow negativity, fearfulness, anger, hatred, deceit, vengeance or any other misguided emotion.

Also, please do not misidentify power and wealth as attributes of a true leader. Although these qualities exist in our society and may even be an asset if used in the right way, true leadership's backbone is comprised solely from pure love. This does not mean you have to be perfect; that is impossible while you are here on Earth. But it does mean you must learn to think with your heart first. Don't get me wrong. Being driven to accomplish, achieve and work hard are not bad characteristics to have. In fact, these types of personality traits can trigger a deeper desire to expand and grow as a human being. What I'm talking about here is on a more personal level, along the lines of a father's *love* for his child. His only goal is to have his child's best interests at *heart*—"love" and "heart" being the operative words here. You can't live without them. The sooner you realize this, the sooner you can lead properly.

Every year, we celebrate Father's Day and Mother's Day. Last year, as part of celebrating Father's Day with my friends and family, including nieces and nephews, grandparents, aunts and uncles, I decided to write a speech. I called it "Happy Man Day". I used the word "man" in general terms, in an attempt to encompass all true leaders. By no means was I intending to minimize the specialness of Father's Day; I simply wished to expand the concept of this specialness to all people who can appreciate the responsibility we all have to each other and to the children of the world. I've included the speech below in the hope that you will better understand what I mean when I encourage you to be a leader, not a follower.

Happy Man Day

Today is a special day. I call it Man Day. Why do I call it Man Day? Because every man in this room has climbed his own mountain and has made it to the top. I know for a fact that every man in this room has helped his fellow man, has protected or is willing to protect a child and has supported and uplifted another human being. And so to the younger generation, as you strike out on your own journeys and encounter your own mountains, remember us men and what we stand for. We are not perfect, but we hope on this beautiful Man Day and until the next Man Day, you learn to live life loving each other. Happy Man Day.

This is only half of the story. To include all the wonderful women out there, **Happy Mother's/Woman's Day** to you, too. Mother Teresa, who was an incredible leader and epitomized what I'm trying to say here, wouldn't have it any other way, I'm sure of it.

Fusing and melting together life's daily experiences with the action of love is not only achievable, it is now mandatory. First, ensure that your mind is capable of hearing and saying the word "LOVE". Then, make sure the mind understands that it is the heart's job to do the rest. The mind can be a great support to pure love. The world uses the mind to do all sorts of wonderful and amazing things. Without it, we would not live as we do, with all this incredible technology around us. That is why it is so important to use our inventions and creations for good in this world. Power and wealth can corrupt if you're not careful. A certain "status" can cloud one's judgment and lead to a sense of superiority. We then treat people as we see fit and ignore those who do not meet our so-called "standards" or who do not coincide with our beliefs. Many governments and powerful people fall into this trap, as they do not understand what the foundation of leadership is. They become consumed with being right and barking orders, and they fail to listen to others of "lesser stature," or they become fogged in with greed.

Can this ever be changed? Can we rely on other people to lead us? YES! And we are the ones to provide the direction—as did Jesus, Buddha, Mother Mary, Krishna, Mahatma Gandhi and Paramahansa Yogananda. And let's not forget current leaders, like Dr. Wayne W. Dyer, Doreen Virtue, Michael Moore and so many others like them. What motivated and motivates them to live as they did and do? It is compassion, which comes from pure love.

Today, you must find it in your heart to love all. No anger or hatred. Let love overcome and surround all the data, all the feelings you have about yourself, other people and any situations you might not agree with. By loving yourself first, you can move outward to love unconditionally your friends, neighbours, community, city and all others who need a blessing this day. It is only when you start to lead in this way that you will see a change in our world, but it does start with you.

Leaders learn to listen to their hearts first. And what a blessing it is when we do.

"Whenever two people meet, there are really six people present. There is each man as he sees himself, each man as the other person sees him, and each man as he really is."

William James

Chapter 9

Control Your Pride and Ego

In the *Gage Canadian Dictionary*, pride is defined as "a high opinion of one's own worth or possessions; too high an opinion of oneself". Ego is defined as "the individual as a whole in his capacity to think, feel and act". The combination of pride and ego working and acting on your behalf conveys an image of a highly opinionated person who feels, acts and reacts in such a way as to maintain the superficial projection of being superior to another. For many, this is a natural reaction when their pride or ego is challenged.

Take a look at all the images we see in magazines and the stories we read in tabloid newspapers. The lust for sensationalism is endless. So much energy is put into outer appearances, and these don't just include looks; they also include status, profession, wealth, nationality and religion. There may be more, but these few examples are perfect to illustrate how pride and ego interact in our daily lives. You can pick any of the above and demonstrate how pride and ego are the masters of those domains.

I'm sure you've heard about instances of really, really wealthy people who appear to have incredible lives, while in reality they are miserable and depressed. What keeps them from seeking help and getting better? Could it be their pride and ego? There are people who have not sought medical attention because of their pride. I'm one of them. I was way too macho to start taking pills for my high blood pressure—until I had no choice. Then, I quickly learned to swallow my pride and ego, along with the pills my doctor prescribed. No pun intended.

So many of us allow pride and ego to get in the way. If we are of a certain race or ethnicity, we always seem to think that our way is the best way. All others fall short. Many nationalities have tied their ethnicity and religion together, generating a belief system of cultural superiority. "We do things this way and that way, and we know this and that, and we are great."

I understand the importance of having pride in your nationality and loving the religion you follow. I, too, was born in a country I love and raised in a religion that introduced me to God, Jesus and the Ten Commandments. Ethnicity, race and religion are not bad things. It's only when pride and ego convince us that ours are better than others' that we begin to run into problems. Problems like war between countries that differ in religion and race. Sure, you can make the argument that war is not about religion or race, but about security, safety and differing ideologies and beliefs. Call it what you want; pride and ego are the ruling factors here. This doesn't mean that both warring factions are at fault. I watch the news and try to stay informed on many of the current topics.

And I understand that there are instigators out there. However, because pride and ego are most certainly present in these types of conflict, it is inevitable that each party will see itself as being right. This creates a vicious and endless circle of head-butting. Take pride and ego out of the equation and replace them with understanding, compassion, reason, fairness and non-judgment, and you will start to see more communication and less fighting.

My son Anthony wrote two poems when he was in grade four. I think they nicely depict what pride and ego bring to the table, versus a world without them. Here they are:

WAR
War sounds like guns shooting incessantly, calling for death
War sounds like your friend saying help
War sounds like you can't move or you'll be shot
War looks like dirt all over you
War looks like bullets whistling through
the air everywhere you look
War tastes like gunpowder burning the back of your throat
War tastes like blood, making you weak
War tastes like friends suffering
War smells like the awful stench of blood
War smells like the war will never end
War smells like you're the only one left

PEACE
Peace smells like flowers blooming
Peace smells like cinnamon buns ready to eat
Peace smells like hot chocolate

Peace feels like you can play outside with your friends
Peace feels like you're safe everywhere you go
Peace feels like you can have lots and lots of friends
Peace tastes like healthy food to eat
Peace tastes like nice cold refreshing water
Peace sounds like a parent, cousins and
friends saying "you can do it"
Peace sounds like the birds chirping
Peace sounds like your mom calling you to "come and eat"
Peace looks like a friend helping you up
Peace looks like a friend letting you have a turn
Peace looks like your mom or dad baking pancakes

On a smaller scale, pride and ego left unchecked can interfere with daily life; relationships are destroyed because of them. You know the old saying, "Sticks and stones will break my bones, but names will never hurt me"? I'm not so sure that's true anymore. The last time I checked, my eight-year-old daughter was very hurt by the names people called her. Pride and ego left to their own devices can and will escalate defence techniques to the proportions we use as adults. Things like road rage, fist fights, trash talk, vengeance, lies, crime, killing and, yes, war. All results of pride and ego.

All confrontational situations involve pride or ego to some degree. Unfortunately, the body, mind and soul suffer. Knowing this, one must practice ensuring pride and ego are NOT at the forefront of confrontations or disagreements. Practice is the key word, though. Every time a situation arises where you think you're right or you feel superior to another—stop and observe yourself.

Observation will make you realize how inflated your ego and pride get when trying to prove a point. You know: those moments when you're in the middle of an argument and you can't let go. You battle to the bitter end. Sometimes, your tactics to win the argument are an all-out attack on a person's character. You'll say anything and everything to show the opponent you are right and they are wrong. How do things get to this point? You guessed it, pride and ego. Need I say more?

So, *observation* of how you react to things is the key. It's very easy to do. In fact, you've already done this almost every time you've argued with someone. In the heat of the battle, you recognize how you're acting, but you don't care. Why? Because pride and ego are very strong. But when you start to actively observe yourself in these moments, the act of observing will significantly distract you from the effects of pride and ego. You actually become captivated with what you are saying. Observing yourself puts you figuratively beside yourself, and you are in awe of the things you say when upset or defensive. For the first time in your life, you start to hear the things you say to people. It's an experience you will never forget. Subsequent arguments now become amusing to you, as you're able to observe more clearly both sides of the argument. Soon, you realize how ridiculous you both sound. Neither party is making sense, so you eventually disengage and decide to bring love to the dispute. And because of your ability to recognize those moments as they are happening, the bouts of anger and tantrums get shorter and shorter, thus allowing you to return to a state of calm. Before you know it, your reaction to most things will have changed—as mine did. It's that simple, and that's exactly how it works.

Remember to recognize the habit of "pride-and-ego reaction" each and every time it happens. Stop and listen to your higher consciousness during these pride-and-ego episodes. It (higher consciousness) does and will speak to you in those moments of uncontrollable emotion. It will show you and remind you how you're acting. Simply observe yourself.

I really don't take stuff personally anymore—not as much as I used to, anyways. Pride and ego aren't as prevalent. If it helps, think of it as the other person's problem that they can't see or hear your side of the story, and simply walk away. This tactic may have a hint of ego in it, but it's a far better approach than fighting to the bitter end until you're declared right or the opponent quits. By the way, do realize that if your opponent quits, it may smell like victory for you, but what's really happening is that your opponent is getting smarter. They are most likely using the observing technique, which is a much healthier way to live. So, never view their quitting as conceding or admitting you were right. This was my mistake. And because I did not learn from this mistake, pride and ego continued to rule me. My beautiful wife so humbly tried to teach me this for many years. She was and is such a strong soul, able to release the argument at hand and teach me at the same time how easy it was to keep the toxins of pride and ego away from the love she had for me. I love you dearly and thank you.

Replace pride and ego with patience and compassion. Patience is defined as "the ability to accept **calmly** things that trouble or annoy, or that require long waiting or effort". Compassion is "feeling for another's sorrow or hardship that leads one **to help** the sufferer". And as a leader, you need to look at the other person across from you, who you are in conflict with, and feel compassion and patience.

Imagine a world where more and more of us live this way. How can there not be a meeting of the minds? This is inevitable. At last, peace.

"A house divided against itself cannot stand."

Abraham Lincoln

Chapter 10

Be Grateful

Magical things happen when you are grateful. Make a habit of being grateful about something each and every day. The more things you can find to be grateful for, the stronger the magic. At some level, it is hard to describe what happens to you after a moment of gratitude. It's as though all your thoughts focus on that part of you which is being grateful, and you become imbued with a feeling of wholeness. The fears and anxiety just seem to disappear.

Life will always have what we perceive as difficulties. And if our perceptions of these difficulties are left unchecked, allowed to grow and flourish in the mind, there will be less and less space for love, peace and calm. So, to make more room for the good in our lives, we must place all things that we can easily be grateful for at the forefront of each and every day.

Affirmations are a perfect example of how some people choose to say and concentrate on things that are good for them. Ask athletes about this. Watching the Olympics and the winning celebrations of these competitors, you will see the thanks they give and the gratitude they have. This raw positive emotion is not by accident. These are young people who have worked hard to get where they are and recognize the ups and downs they had to go through to achieve their goals. Even the ones who don't win medals can be found being humble, happy and grateful for the experience.

All of us need to practice this transforming habit. It truly does carry you through the good times and bad. When all is said and done, and you are left standing there in gratitude for the good in your life, you will find no room within for the things you perceive as bad. Gratefulness does not allow negativity in. This is the magic.

In this life, you have a choice: to be grateful or to be unhappy. When you stay in the mode of unhappiness, you are essentially practicing the habit that is opposite to being grateful. It's time to start practicing the habit of gratitude. You will soon see how easy it is to get yourself into a happy state of mind. Like anything that is new and unfamiliar, it takes hard work to see results. Thankfully, the way the human mind, body and soul were designed, we are able to compute, feel and know immediately whether what we are doing is right or wrong, feels good or not, and whether what we are doing is benefiting us. So, let your internal guidance mechanism lead the way. Become aware of how you are thinking, and swap the unhappy thoughts for ones of gratitude.

There are a lot of people in this world who live in poverty and hardship. My words about gratitude might even seem offensive to some. We never know what it is like to walk in another person's shoes until we actually do. Gratitude does not change your living conditions; it changes how you feel and see yourself. Self-worth is important, and gratitude will show you who you really are: worthy of God's love and all the gifts life has to offer.

I must admit, I am fortunate to have a roof over my head, food on the table and a safe, clean environment to live in. I have practiced being grateful, though, and I can honestly say that it has lifted me up. I'm not suggesting that my past was more dire than another's, or that I understand everybody's situation. What I'm trying to convey here is that when you give gratitude, no matter the circumstances, life hears you, God hears you and, most importantly, you hear yourself being strong, humble, happier and loving. Nothing can take this away from you.

Our world—me, you and all the people of Earth—need to hear, more often, the voice of gratitude. Something divine happens when that one person in the room turns the conversation to things we can be grateful for. Everyone starts to agree. At those moments, we should really make the effort to absorb the energy gratitude brings. Stop so you can really hear and feel the thanks being poured out from the heart. This is where true power comes from. Without it, we lose ourselves into nothingness. Life can become shallow, full of empty words, thoughts and actions.

Prevent yourself from falling asleep. Life is about living, and to live you must be of the heart. In the heart, you will find *love*, *gratitude* and *compassion*. You must never be embarrassed about these traits. Nourish them and you will find out where life's journey is taking you. We are all going in the same direction.

"I am with you always."

God

Conclusion

Master Chapters One Through Ten

Positivity is the *only* way out of negativity.

Meditate.

Break on through to the other side.

Always have faith, no matter what.

It's easy to be mean. It's easier to be nice.

Let go and let God.

Pray always.

Become a leader, not a follower.

Control your pride and ego.

Be grateful.

Feels like a lot of work there, doesn't it? Well, I can tell you this: these past eight years have blown by. I haven't mastered any of the above, but the past eight years have been transformative. I continue to work on myself and live by the principles in this book. You've now heard me say and repeat that I'm not perfect and I don't expect myself to be. But in the words of my spiritual guru, Dr. Wayne W. Dyer: "I'm better than I used to be." This is all life asks of you.

At the age of forty-two and with a journey of contemplation, practice and reflection under my belt, I can say that things are much clearer to me. Gone are the days of youthful naiveté—not that there is anything wrong with this. It's just that I realize now, more than ever, the beautiful gift we have been given, which has been laid at our feet for us to accept, embrace and expand with. That gift is *life*, mistakes and all. But now, as you move through life, you truly see each "mistake" as an opportunity. Evolving to a "higher level" happens twice as quickly if you are willing to see your mistakes as opportunities to grow, as precious things no amount of money can buy. Best of all, they're free.

All the craziness and drama we manage to find ourselves in are distractions from life's purpose. Sure, we all have to live and learn. There are always going to be things that challenge you, be those anger issues, addictions, health challenges, fear, anxiety, boredom and so on. These have been placed in your life to learn from and grow as a person, and I think most of us are doing a fantastic job. My hope is that this book ignites the spark in you that will light your way to the next level.

I am living proof that one can go from feeling less than ordinary as a human to knowing that you, me, us, we are all extraordinary people. I try to live from that place each and every day. Those who know me or who will get to know me might think I'm crazy at times. The visions I have for this world and the goals and aspirations I place in front of me all come from a passion for Mother Earth and the human race. And when you listen carefully, the message is always about LOVE.

Some people have told me, "One person cannot change anything in this world." I'm still not sure whether I agree with that, but for what it's worth, it is not our destiny to change the *whole* world. That is why I have written this book. It holds the secrets to what I have learned in my life regarding change—most importantly, that you must love yourself first. You can't just say you love yourself; you need to learn how and to what level you must love. Then and only then will *your world* change.

All of this comes from within, deep down into the depths of you and your soul. In this location, you will find peace and calm. When that is located—through hard work and determination— you can begin to expand outward, giving back what was once placed at your feet freely and lovingly.

I'm not missing out on life. I'm breathing in every God-made molecule of air I can. My life did not end when the party was over; it began. I lost nothing from this awakening and received everything. Do you lose when you are free? *A Course in Miracles* answers this poetically: "Until you realize you give up nothing, until you understand there is no loss . . . you will not see the many gains your choice has offered you. Yet though you do not see them, they are there."

What I'm trying to tell you, and what many of the self-help books are trying to tell you, is that there is a way to peace and joy.

If the desire is there, or you realize a change is needed in how you are, then you—with the support and encouragement of God, all the angels in Heaven, Jesus, Mother Mary, all the saints and any loved ones who have passed on—must take that first step. This is all that is needed; the rest of the journey becomes a mystical and magical time of ups and downs, lessons realized, evolution, growth, wisdom, courage, leadership, strength and so on, but never failure.

When the fear of loss is gone, you will awaken. When you start to use the words "I don't think I need this anymore", whether in reference to booze or drugs or anger or stress, then you are well on your way.

God blesses you, Student of Life. Go in peace, and attain what is divinely yours.

And in the words of a most wise person, my little Karina, who gives me unconditional love each and every day, I LOVE YOU ALL.